MEXICO, CENTRAL AMERICA, AND THE CARIBBEAN

There are dry deserts in northern Mexico and wet rain forests in Central America. Not many creatures are able to survive in the scorching desert, but an amazing number of animals and plants live in tropical rain forests. To the east, the Caribbean Sea is famous for its coral reefs, which are home to a colorful collection of marine creatures.

Rhinoceros iguana

BAHAMAS

West Indian flamingo

Atlantic Ocean

Spotted dolphin

Stingray

CUBA

JAMAICA

Jamaican white peacock butterfly

HAITI

DOMINICAN REPUBLIC

Marine toad

Frigate bird

HONDURAS

West Indian manatee

Green turtle

Caribbean reef shark

Caribbean Sea

Sisserou parrot

NICARAGUA

Swordfish

Puffer fish

St. Vincent parrot

Keel-billed toucan

Clown fish

White-tail sabre wing hummingbird

PANAMA

Howler monkey

Spider monkey

0   1000km

0   500 miles

ROCKY DESERT

The deserts of the western U.S. are very dry and hot. Not many plants can grow in these harsh conditions. The animals that survive in this habitat have special ways of hunting and of protecting themselves from the fierce heat.

When it is attacked, the **western banded gecko** can deliberately "lose" its tail. The predator eats the tail while the gecko runs away.

When the **chuckwalla** hides between rocks, it puffs out its body so that it cannot be dragged out by a predator.

The **greater roadrunner** is the size of a chicken. It can run at 25 miles per hour (40 km/hr).

When a **western diamondback rattlesnake** shakes its tail, the tip rattles!

The **Gila monster** is a dangerous lizard. It squirts poison through its teeth.

Desert tortoise

12

The **golden eagle** soars high up above the desert and then swoops down at great speed to catch its prey.

The **red-tailed hawk** has excellent eyesight. It can see its prey moving from far away.

Painted lady butterfly

The **Mojave ground squirrel** sleeps in a burrow during the hottest months of the summer.

Mojave sootywing butterfly

Tarantula hawk wasp

The **desert rosy boa** is a snake that eats small animals and birds. It rolls up in a ball when it is attacked.

Desert tarantula

Rough harvester ants

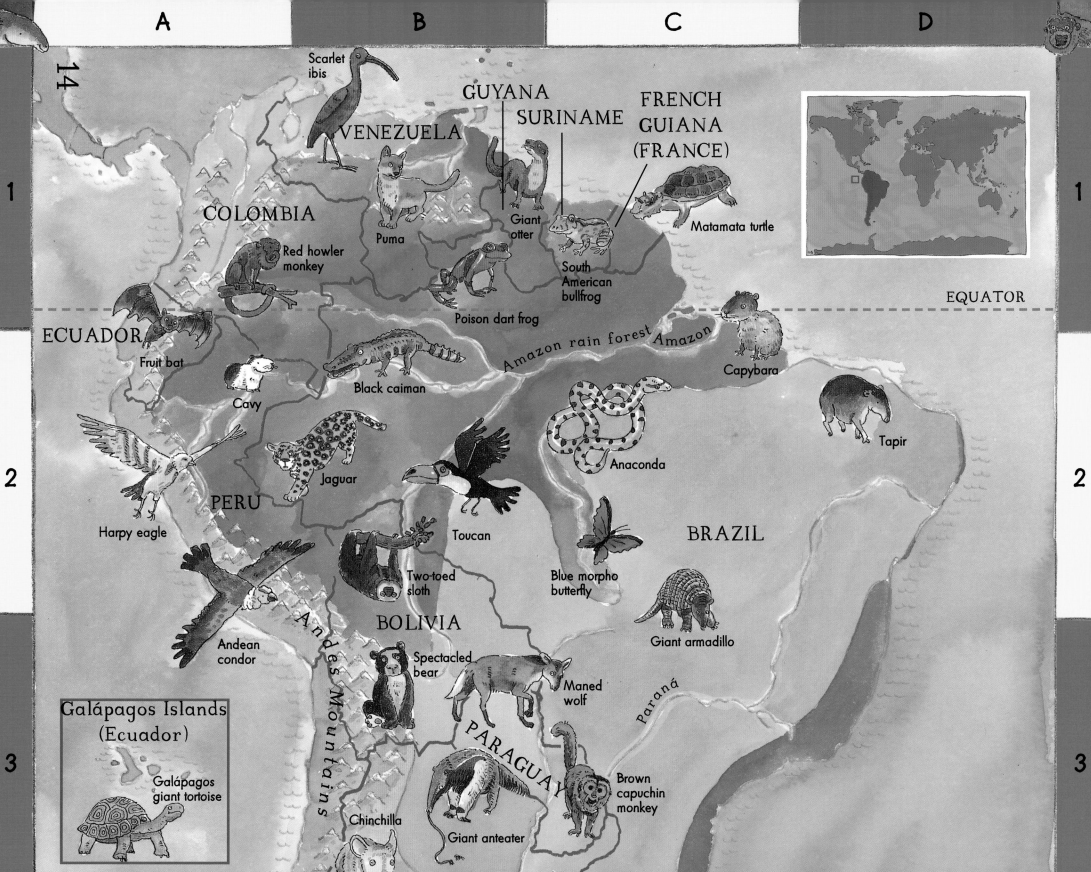

Scarlet ibis

GUYANA
SURINAME
VENEZUELA
FRENCH GUIANA (FRANCE)

COLOMBIA

Puma

Giant otter

Matamata turtle

Red howler monkey

South American bullfrog

EQUATOR

ECUADOR

Fruit bat

Poison dart frog

Amazon rain forest Amazon

Cavy

Black caiman

Capybara

Jaguar

Anaconda

Tapir

PERU

Harpy eagle

Toucan

BRAZIL

Two-toed sloth

Blue morpho butterfly

Giant armadillo

Andean condor

BOLIVIA

Spectacled bear

Maned wolf

Paraná

Galápagos Islands (Ecuador)

Galápagos giant tortoise

PARAGUAY

Brown capuchin monkey

Chinchilla

Giant anteater

Andes Mountains

Pacific Ocean

ARGENTINA

Sheep

URUGUAY

Atlantic Ocean

Alpaca

Rhea

CHILE

Cattle

Pampas deer

Patagonia

Falkland Islands (U.K.)

Fur seal

Magellanic penguin

Sea lion

Sardines

SOUTH AMERICA

South America has a variety of habitats. The Amazon rain forest contains more species than anywhere else on Earth. The Andes, the world's longest mountain range, is home to many different animals. The southern grasslands are also rich in wildlife.

The **Andean condor** is one of the world's heaviest flying birds, weighing up to 33 pounds (15 kilograms). Amazingly, it can spot another condor 6 miles (9 kilometers) away.

Can you find one?

0   1000km

0   500 miles

RAIN FOREST

The Amazon rain forest is very hot and also extremely wet—it rains for around 250 days each year. This combination is perfect for both plant and animal life, and this is why the rain forest is home to so many different species.

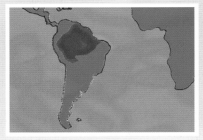

The colorful beak of the **toco toucan** is almost as big as the bird itself. It is mostly made of lightweight bone.

Blue morpho butterflies have bright blue wings. They flash when they catch the sunlight.

The **black caiman** is a big, dangerous alligator that preys on large animals, including humans.

Green iguana

The steamy rain forest climate is ideal for frogs. The **poison dart frog** has bright colors to warn predators to stay away.

Longhorn beetles have two antennae that can be longer than their bodies.

Scarlet macaw

Red howler monkeys

Tree kinkajou

The **two-toed sloth** eats, sleeps, and even gives birth upside down!

Emerald tree boa

The world's largest rodent is the **capybara**. It is more than 3 feet (1 meter) long and almost 20 inches (50 centimeters) tall.

The spotted fur of the **jaguar** helps it hide in the shadows of the rain forest.

The strange **matamata turtle** snaps up small creatures as they float or swim by.

Giant otters can stay underwater for several minutes. Their sensitive whiskers help them find prey in the murky river.

17

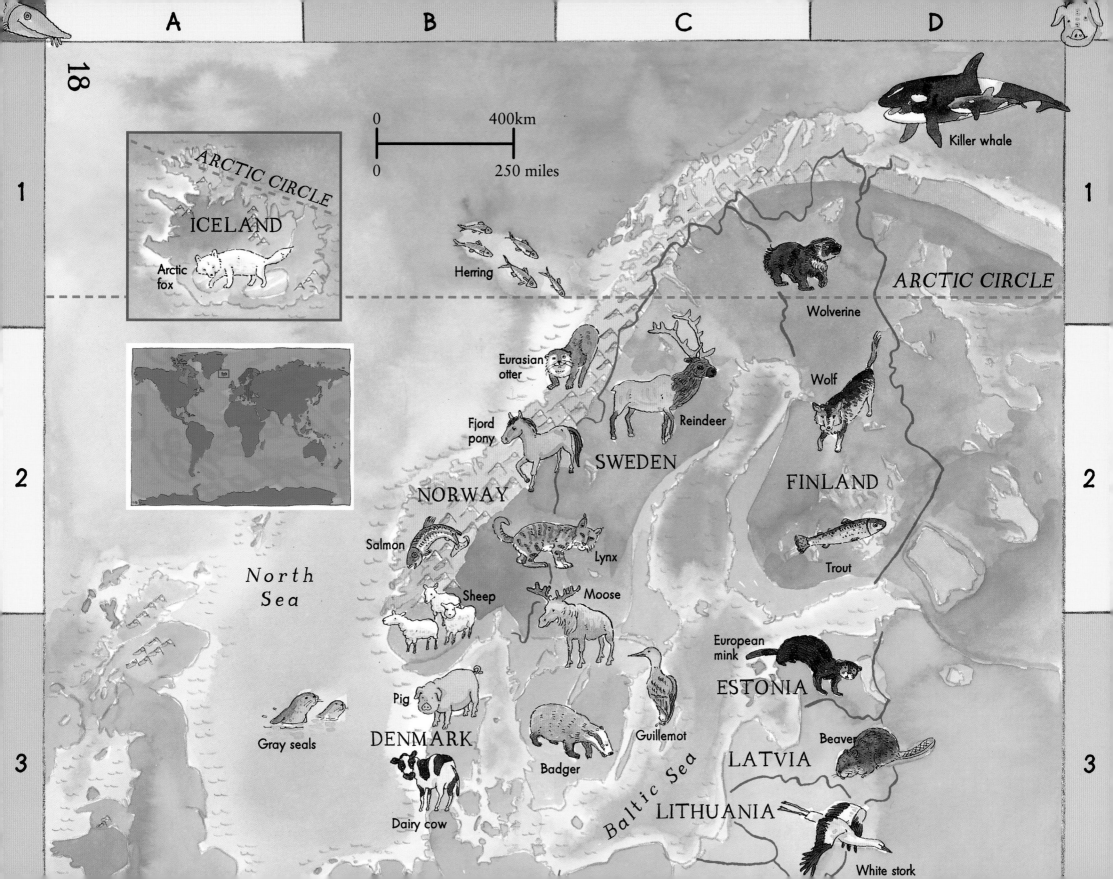

Killer whale

ARCTIC CIRCLE

ICELAND

Arctic fox

0   400km

0   250 miles

Herring

Wolverine

ARCTIC CIRCLE

Eurasian otter

Reindeer

Wolf

Fjord pony

SWEDEN

FINLAND

NORWAY

Salmon

Lynx

Trout

North Sea

Sheep

Moose

European mink

Pig

ESTONIA

Gray seals

DENMARK

Badger

Guillemot

Beaver

LATVIA

Dairy cow

Baltic Sea

LITHUANIA

White stork

The **reindeer** of northern parts of Norway and Sweden are always on the move in search of food. Large herds swim across freezing rivers and even through the sea between islands.

Can you find one on the map?

Vistula

European bison

CZECH REPUBLIC

POLAND

Deer

Tiger moth

Muskrat

Heron

Danube

SLOVAKIA

European hare

Ibex

HUNGARY

SLOVENIA

ROMANIA

CROATIA

Deer

Wild boar

BOSNIA & HERZEGOVINA

Danube

Black Sea

Sturgeon

Garden dormouse

SERBIA

BULGARIA

MONTENEGRO

Brown bear

ALBANIA

NORTH MACEDONIA

Lesser horseshoe bat

Goat

Marginated tortoise

GREECE

Bottle-nosed dolphin

Mediterranean Sea

NORTHERN AND EASTERN EUROPE

Animals that live in the north of Europe survive well in the cold, snowy pine forests and mountains. Farther south, the climate is warmer, and there is a greater variety of animal species. The wildlife that lives close to the Mediterranean Sea is well suited to that hot climate.

1   1

WESTERN EUROPE

Europe is a small continent with many different animal habitats. Wildlife is found everywhere, from cool, shady woodlands to hot, dry plains. Animals have also adapted to life in the high mountains of central and southern Europe.

Gray seal

Gray squirrels were brought to the U.K. from the U.S. in the 1800s. They are now more common than the smaller red squirrel.

Can you find one on the map?

2   2

Haddock

Highland cattle

Cod

North Sea

Baltic Sea

SCOTLAND

UNITED KINGDOM

NORTHERN IRELAND

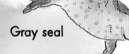

Gray squirrel

NETHERLANDS

3   3

Horse

Sheep

Plaice

Avocet

Western European hedgehog

IRELAND

4

Red fox

Rhine

GERMANY

White stork

BELGIUM

Deer

LUXEMBOURG

Great white heron

Seine

European hare

Danube

Wild boar

Atlantic Ocean

Brown crab

Loire

Cow

FRANCE

Eurasian lynx

Alps

AUSTRIA

SWITZERLAND

LIECHTENSTEIN

5

Goose

Po

Oysters

ANDORRA

Wild horse

Rhône

Chamois

Crested porcupine

Ibex

MONACO

SAN MARINO

Pyrenees

Griffon vulture

ITALY

Pilchards

Bull

Ebro

Sardines

CORSICA (FRANCE)

Honey buzzard

Apollo butterfly

BALEARIC ISLANDS (SPAIN)

Crayfish

Bobtail squid

Prawn

PORTUGAL

Tagus

SARDINIA (ITALY)

SPAIN

Common genet

Greater flamingo

White-spotted octopus

Swordfish

6

GIBRALTAR (U.K.)

Anchovies

SICILY (ITALY)

MALTA

Mediterranean Sea

21

Tuna

0   400km

European lobster

0   250 miles

A   B   C   D

WOODLAND

Trees that lose their leaves in the winter are called deciduous. Woods of deciduous trees, like this one in Europe, are home to many different animals, birds, and insects. Each woodland creature has a special job to do, such as spreading seeds.

Long-eared bat

Only the male **blackbird** is black—the female is brown. Blackbirds eat insects, worms, and berries.

Garden spider

Red admiral butterfly

Common shrew

The **adder** likes t bask in the sun in woodland clearing

The **red fox** usually hunts at night. It eats nuts and berries, as well as small forest creatures.

Earthworm

22

Green woodpecker

Tawny owl

In fall, the **gray squirrel** buries food underground. It digs it up again in the winter.

A **robin** fights other robins in order to protect its territory. It will even attack its own reflection!

Badger

The **garden snail** retreats into its shell when the weather is dry. It can then live for several months without water.

Wood mouse

The **hedgehog** is usually active at night. During the day, it curls into a ball to sleep.

Wood lice

23

RUSSIA AND ITS NEIGHBORS

Russia is a huge country, and the wildlife is as varied as the landscape. Frozen tundra, pine forests, and mountain ranges are home to many different creatures. In countries south of Russia, the climate is drier, and tough animals survive in the high-lying deserts.

Arctic Ocean

Collared lemming

Polar bear

Yenisey

Arctic cod

Canada goose

ARCTIC CIRCLE

Lynx

Moose

Golden eagle

Reindeer

Ural Mountains

Russian flying squirrel

Ob

Steppe polecat

KALININGRAD

Volga

Honeybee

Snow leopard

Red fox

Domestic pig

BELARUS

Ural

Saiga antelope

KAZAKHSTAN

Wild boar

UKRAINE

Chamois

Bactrian camel

MOLDOVA

Caspian seal

Black Sea

Caspian Sea

GEORGIA

ARMENIA

UZBEKISTAN

KYRGYZSTAN

TAJIKISTAN

AZERBAIJAN

Jackal

TURKMENISTAN

24

1

Wolves live in pine forests. Their dark fur hides them in the shadows, helping them to catch prey.

Can you find one?

Beluga whale

Narwhal

2

Ringed seal

Brown bear

Snow goose

S i b e r i a

Walrus

Siberian deer

Wolf

Lena

Siberian salamander

Bearded seal

3

R U S S I A

Siberian hamster

Sea lion

Amur

Siberian tiger

Crested puffin

Pacific Ocean

4

Sperm whale

0   1000km

0   500 miles

25

1

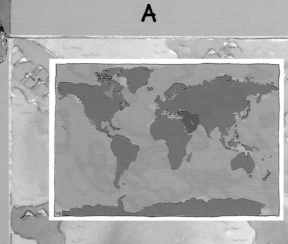

Angora goat

Brown bear

Thermit ibis

TURKEY

Wild sheep

Sand gazelles

SYRIA

CYPRUS

2

Mediterranean Sea

LEBANON

Wild boar

ISRAEL

JORDAN

Turkish gecko

Dromedary camel

SOUTHWESTERN ASIA

Mountain ranges lie to the northeast of this region, but much of southwestern Asia is extremely dry and hot. The deserts in this part of the world are sandy and windy. Few animals can survive in the scorching heat. Those that do are able to live on very little water.

Fennec fox

Dugong

3

Hamadryas baboon

Tiger shark

Red Sea

The **dromedary camel** can go without water for a week. When it does drink, it can gulp down up to 52 gallons (200 liters) of water in one go.

Hawksbill turtle

Can you find one on the map?

4

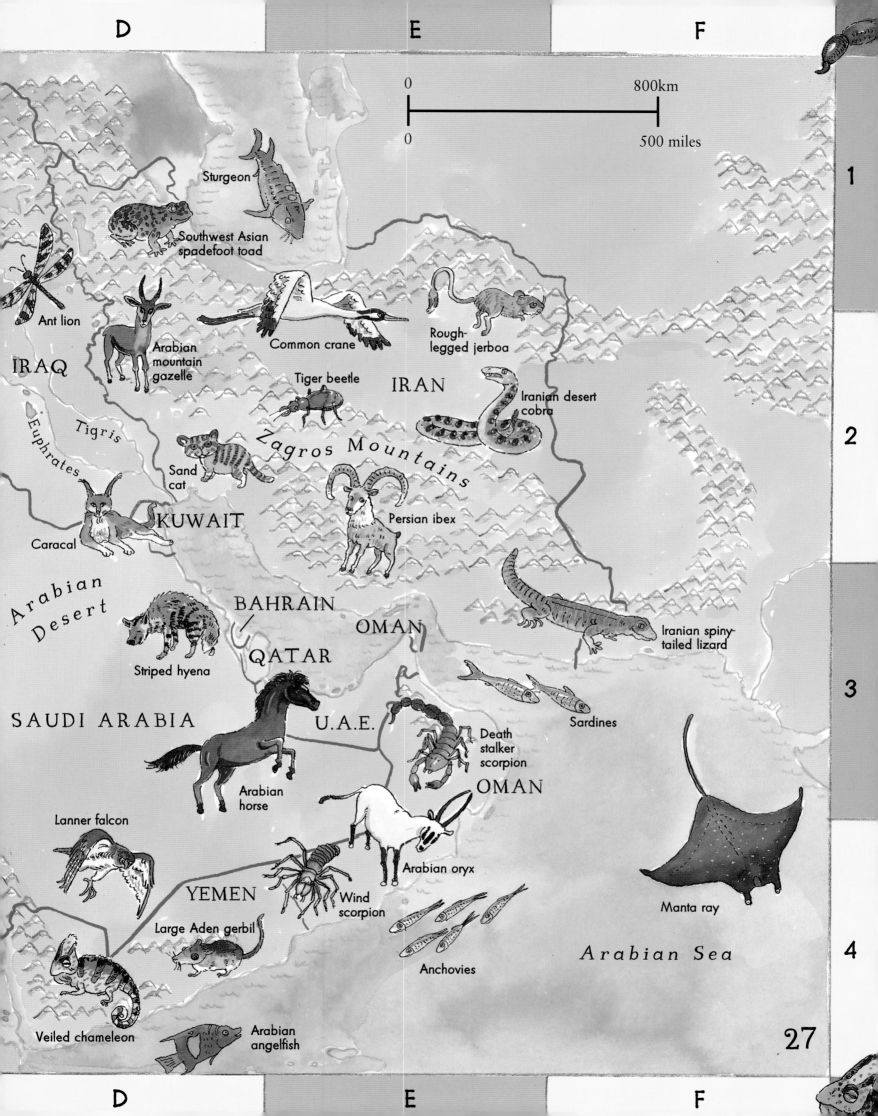

D

E

F

0   800km

0   500 miles

1

Sturgeon

Southwest Asian
spadefoot toad

Ant lion

Arabian
mountain
gazelle

Common crane

Rough-
legged jerboa

IRAQ

Tigris

Tiger beetle

IRAN

Iranian desert
cobra

2

Euphrates

Sand
cat

Zagros Mountains

Caracal

KUWAIT

Persian ibex

*Arabian
Desert*

Striped hyena

BAHRAIN

QATAR

OMAN

Iranian spiny-
tailed lizard

3

SAUDI ARABIA

U.A.E.

Death
stalker
scorpion

Sardines

Arabian
horse

OMAN

Lanner falcon

Arabian oryx

YEMEN

Wind
scorpion

Manta ray

Large Aden gerbil

4

Anchovies

Arabian Sea

Veiled chameleon

Arabian
angelfish

27

D

E

F

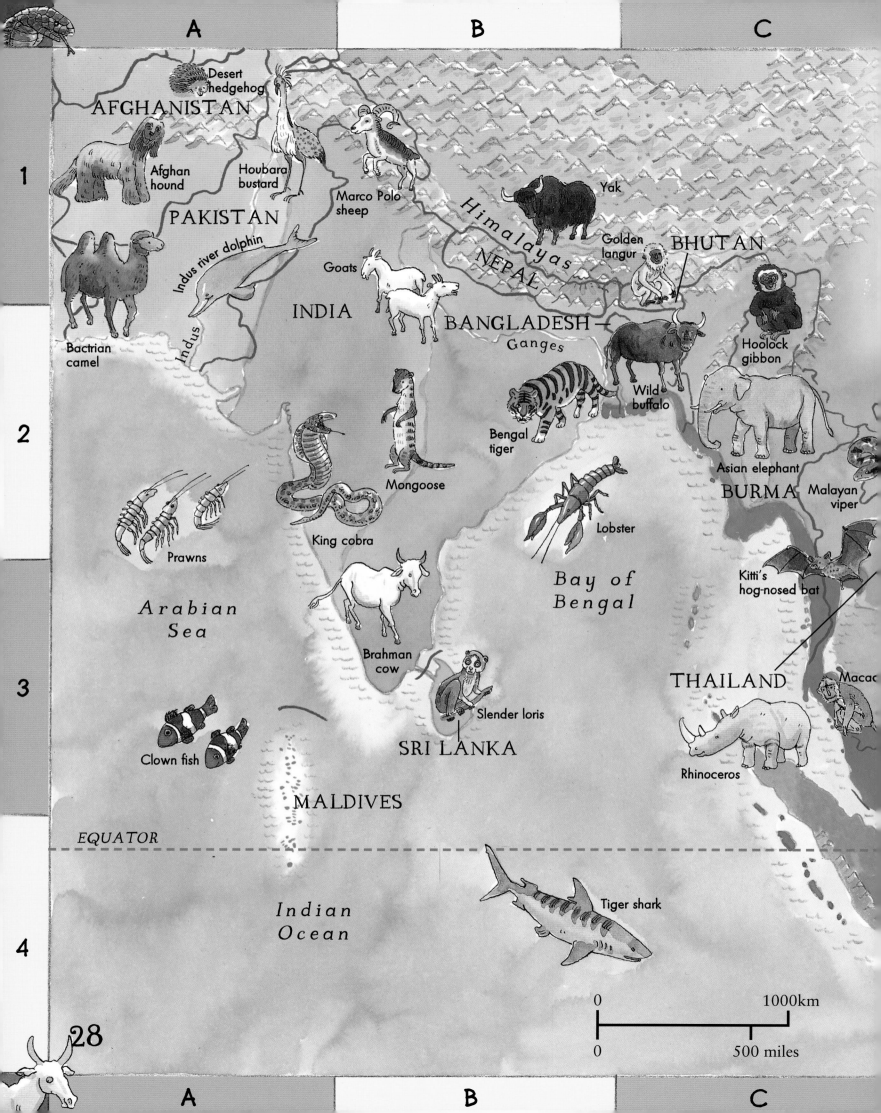

A

B

C

1

Desert hedgehog

AFGHANISTAN

Afghan hound

Houbara bustard

Marco Polo sheep

PAKISTAN

Yak

Himalayas

BHUTAN

Golden langur

NEPAL

Bactrian camel

Indus river dolphin

Indus

Goats

INDIA

BANGLADESH

Ganges

Hoolock gibbon

2

Wild buffalo

Bengal tiger

Asian elephant

BURMA

Malayan viper

Mongoose

King cobra

Lobster

Prawns

Bay of Bengal

Kitti's hog-nosed bat

Arabian Sea

Brahman cow

Clown fish

Slender loris

THAILAND

Macac

3

SRI LANKA

Rhinoceros

MALDIVES

EQUATOR

Indian Ocean

Tiger shark

4

0   1000km

28

0   500 miles

A

B

C

SOUTHERN AND SOUTHEASTERN ASIA

A huge mountain range called the Himalayas lies to the north of this region. Countries south of the Himalayas are very hot, and those close to the equator have a tropical climate. Most of Indonesia is covered with thick rain forest, which is home to a wide variety of wildlife.

1

The **Komodo dragon** is the world's biggest lizard, and it looks like a living dinosaur. It grows up to 10 feet (3 meters) long.

Can you find one?

2

Asiatic black bear

VIETNAM

South China Sea

Draco lizard

LAOS

Clouded leopard

Manta ray

PHILIPPINES

CAMBODIA

MALAYSIA

3

Pacific Ocean

SINGAPORE

Tarsier

Philippine cockatoo

Hornbill

BRUNEI

Giant palm civet

Leatherback turtle

Orangutans

INDONESIA

4

Queen Alexandra birdwing butterfly

Malayan tapir

Komodo dragon

EAST TIMOR

THE HIMALAYAS

The Himalayas form the biggest range, or group, of mountains in the world. Fourteen of the world's tallest mountains are found in the Himalayas. The sturdy animals that live there are well adapted to life on the high slopes.

Musk deer

The **bharal** lives in small herds and is preyed on by snow leopards.

The **Himalayan brown bear** lives high up the mountain in the summer, when it is not too cold to survive up there.

Himalayan weasel

Himalayan pika

When a male **rock agama** fights another male, he will try to hit the other lizard on the head with his tail!

The **bearded vulture** builds its nest high up on craggy mountain rocks. It feeds on dead animals, dropping the bones in order to smash them and get to the tasty marrow inside.

Red-billed blue magpie

Himalayan yellow-throated marten

The **yak** is a wild mountain ox. It climbs around 20,000 feet (6,100 meters) up the mountain to feed. An adult male can weigh as much as ten humans.

Marmot

Snow leopards can live higher up than any other wildcat. When they sleep, they wrap their tails around their bodies to stay warm.

Swallowtail butterfly

The male **Himalayan monal pheasant** is brightly colored and has a crest of feathers on its head. The smaller female has no crest and is brown in color.

31

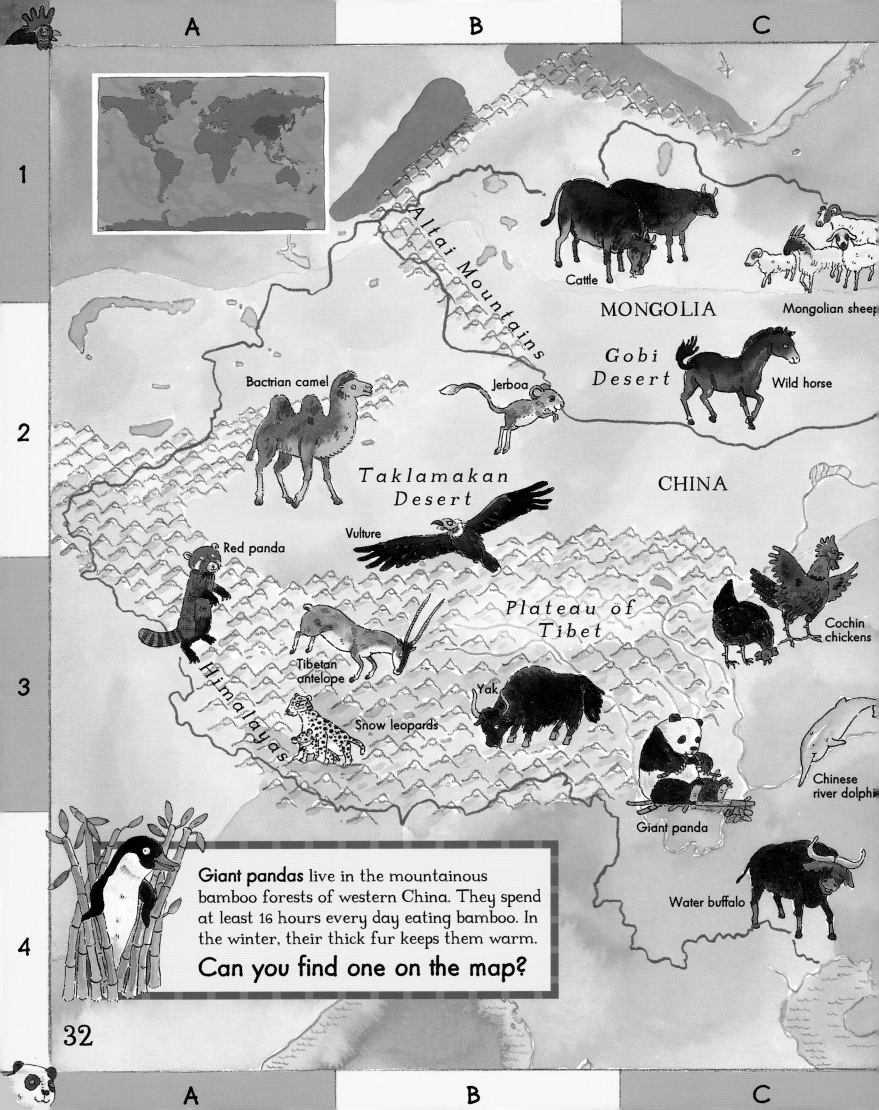

A   B   C

1

2

3

4

Altai Mountains

Cattle

MONGOLIA

Mongolian sheep

Gobi Desert

Bactrian camel

Jerboa

Wild horse

Taklamakan Desert

CHINA

Vulture

Red panda

Plateau of Tibet

Cochin chickens

Himalayas

Tibetan antelope

Yak

Snow leopards

Giant panda

Chinese river dolphin

Water buffalo

Giant pandas live in the mountainous bamboo forests of western China. They spend at least 16 hours every day eating bamboo. In the winter, their thick fur keeps them warm.

Can you find one on the map?

32

A   B   C

1

0   1000km

0   500 miles

Black bear

Nen Jiang

Siberian tiger

Dhole

Harlequin duck

House swallow

2

Steller's sea eagle

NORTH KOREA

Squid

Whooper swan

Japanese macaque

SOUTH KOREA

Pacific Ocean

Huang He (Yellow river)

Crane

JAPAN

Siberian musk deer

Chinese alligator

3

Octopus

CHINA AND JAPAN

Chang Jiang (Yangtze)

Chinese moon moth

Emerald green tree frog

As well as having the world's biggest human population, China is also home to many amazing species of wild animals. A wide variety of creatures live in the mountains to the south and the high-lying deserts to the north. The seas around Japan and North and South Korea are full of interesting marine life.

Gibbon

TAIWAN

Unicorn beetle

4

Dugong

33

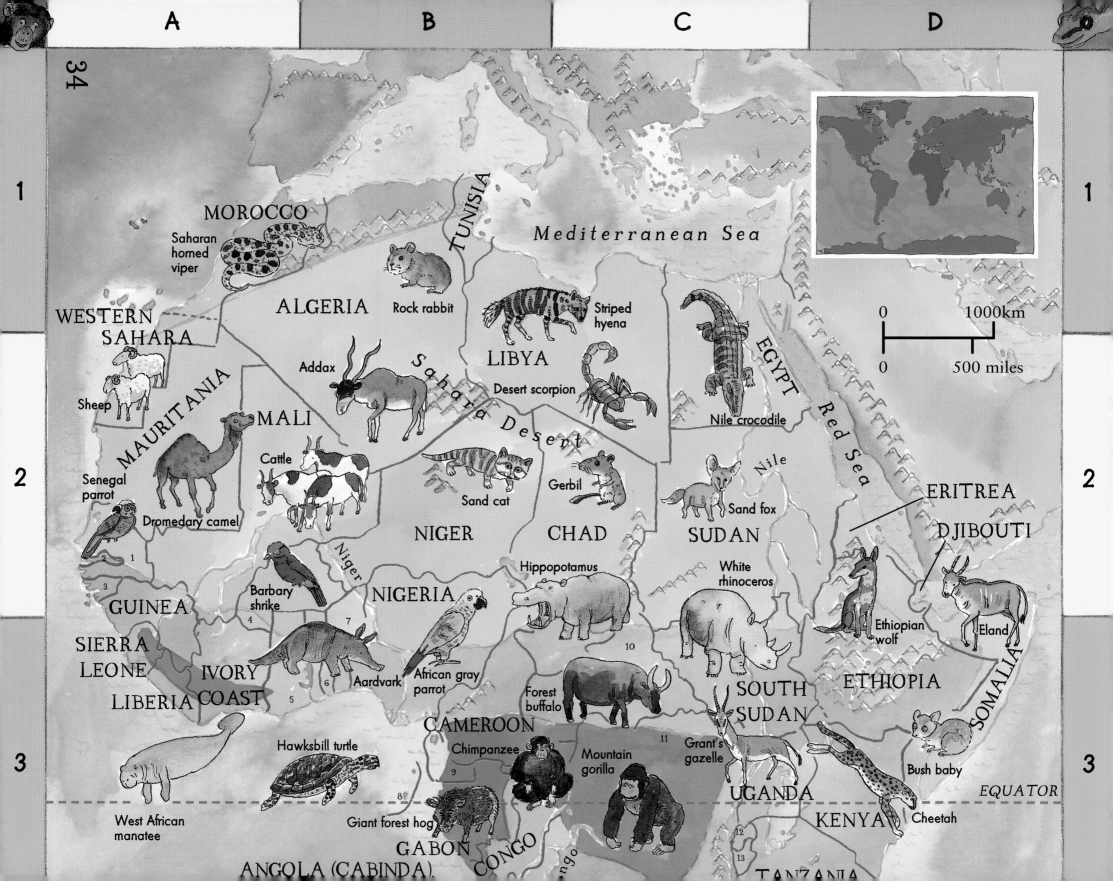

1

MOROCCO

Saharan
horned
viper

Mediterranean Sea

TUNISIA

ALGERIA

Rock rabbit

WESTERN
SAHARA

Striped
hyena

LIBYA

EGYPT

Red Sea

Sheep

Addax

Sahara Desert

Desert scorpion

Nile crocodile

MAURITANIA

MALI

1000km

500 miles

2

Cattle

Senegal
parrot

Dromedary camel

Sand cat

Gerbil

Sand fox

Nile

ERITREA

DJIBOUTI

NIGER

CHAD

SUDAN

1

Niger

Barbary
shrike

NIGERIA

Hippopotamus

White
rhinoceros

Ethiopian
wolf

GUINEA

4

7

Eland

SIERRA
LEONE

Aardvark

African gray
parrot

10

Forest
buffalo

ETHIOPIA

IVORY
COAST

6

SOUTH
SUDAN

SOMALIA

LIBERIA

5

CAMEROON

11

Grant's
gazelle

Hawksbill turtle

Chimpanzee

Mountain
gorilla

Bush baby

9

UGANDA

3

West African
manatee

8

Giant forest hog

KENYA

Cheetah

EQUATOR

GABON

CONGO

12

ANGOLA (CABINDA)

13

TANZANIA

EQUATOR

Key to African countries:

1 SENEGAL
2 THE GAMBIA
3 GUINEA-BISSAU
4 BURKINA FASO
5 GHANA
6 TOGO
7 BENIN
8 SÃO TOME & PRINCIPE
9 EQUATORIA GUINEA
10 CENTRAL AFRICAN REPUBLIC
11 DEMOCRATIC REPUBLIC OF THE CONGO
12 RWANDA
13 BURUNDI
14 MALAWI
15 ZIMBABWE

Atlantic Ocean

African elephant

Colobus monkey

ZAMBIA

COMOROS

Crested hornbill

African wild dogs

ANGOLA

Leopard

Zambezi

Ring-tailed lemur

14

15

Gecko

MOZAMBIQUE

MADAGASCAR

NAMIBIA

Savanna baboon

Kalahari lion

Shrimps

Zebra

BOTSWANA

Giraffe

Jackson's chameleon

ESWATINI (SWAZILAND)

Sardines

Springbok

LESOTHO

SOUTH AFRICA

Indian Ocean

South African porcupine

Herring

AFRICA

The enormous continent of Africa is home to a fantastic variety of wildlife. Some amazing animals live on grasslands south of the Sahara desert. In western Africa, tropical rain forests shelter many unusual and rare creatures. Farther south, animals survive in the dry bush and hot desert.

Desert scorpions get all their water from their food. They eat insects and spiders. Baby scorpions ride on their mother's back, underneath her deadly sting.

Can you find one on the map?

SAVANNA

The vast grassy plains of Africa are called the savanna. Herds of wild animals, such as gazelles, live in this habitat. They are hunted by lions and other predators.

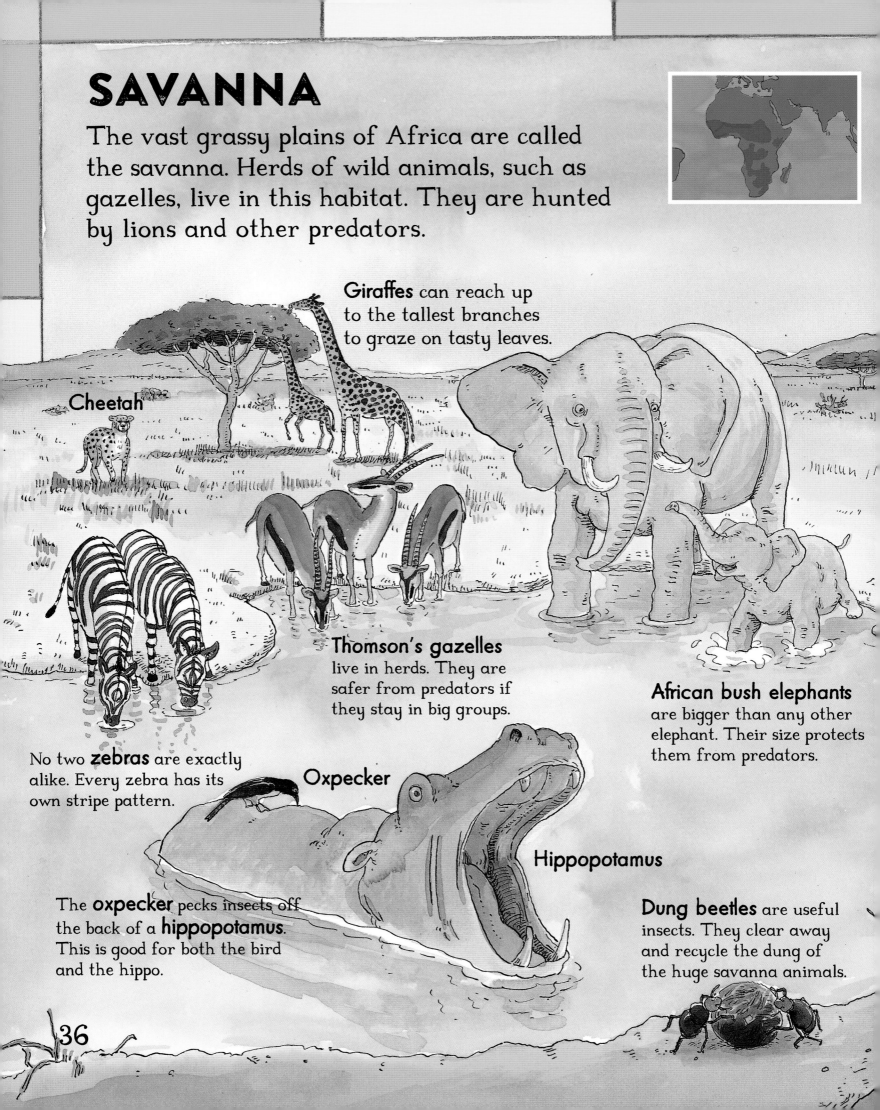

Giraffes can reach up to the tallest branches to graze on tasty leaves.

Cheetah

Thomson's gazelles live in herds. They are safer from predators if they stay in big groups.

No two **zebras** are exactly alike. Every zebra has its own stripe pattern.

Oxpecker

African bush elephants are bigger than any other elephant. Their size protects them from predators.

Hippopotamus

The **oxpecker** pecks insects off the back of a **hippopotamus**. This is good for both the bird and the hippo.

Dung beetles are useful insects. They clear away and recycle the dung of the huge savanna animals.

The **griffon vulture** never kills its own food. It eats the meat of animals that are already dead.

Savanna baboons

Eastern black-white colobus monkeys shelter from the heat in the shady branches of a tree.

A male **lion** does not hunt as much as a female does. Lions live in groups called prides.

If a **pangolin** is in danger, it rolls up into a ball.

Black rhinoceroses come to water holes to drink.

The tusks of a male **warthog** can grow up to 25 inches (64 centimeters) long.

The **savanna monitor lizard** flicks its forked tongue in and out to find prey. It eats birds, snakes, lizards, and eggs.

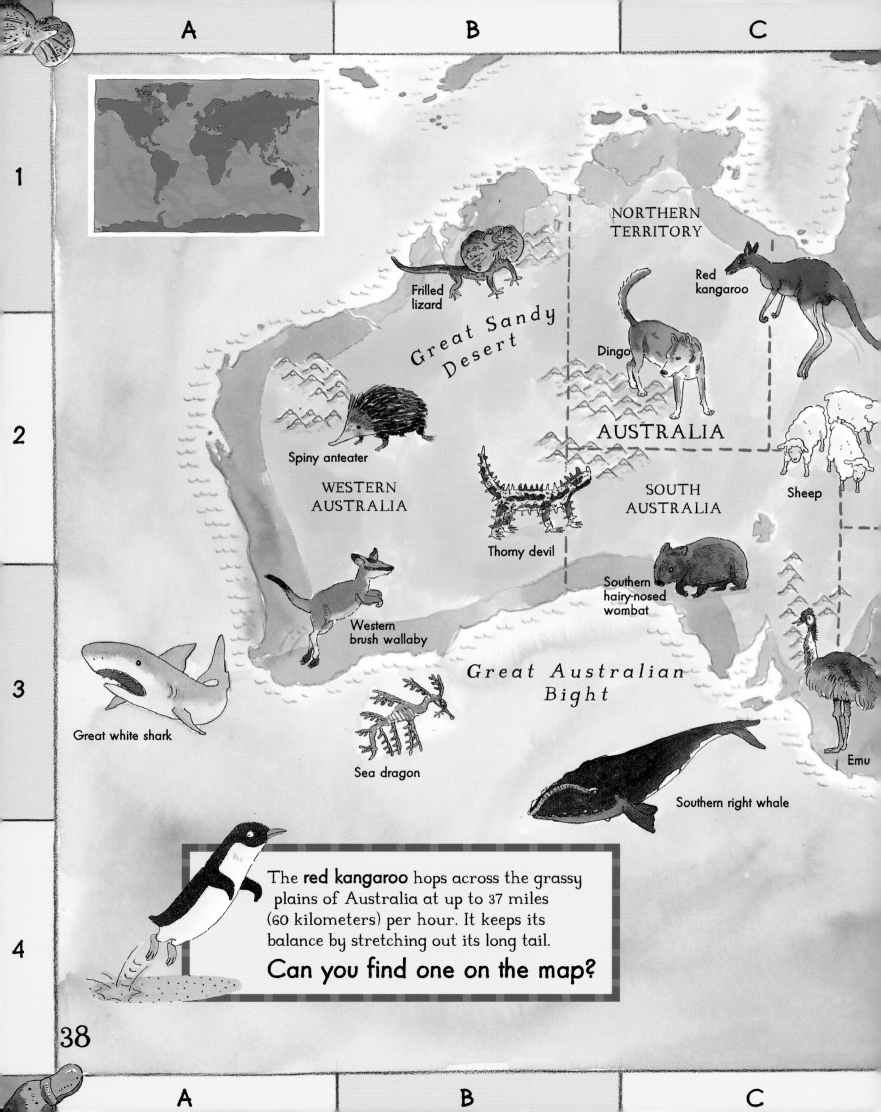

1

Frilled
lizard

NORTHERN
TERRITORY

Red
kangaroo

Great Sandy
Desert

Dingo

AUSTRALIA

2

Spiny anteater

WESTERN
AUSTRALIA

SOUTH
AUSTRALIA

Sheep

Thorny devil

Southern
hairy-nosed
wombat

Western
brush wallaby

Great Australian
Bight

3

Great white shark

Sea dragon

Southern right whale

Emu

4

The **red kangaroo** hops across the grassy
plains of Australia at up to 37 miles
(60 kilometers) per hour. It keeps its
balance by stretching out its long tail.

Can you find one on the map?

1

AUSTRALIA AND NEW ZEALAND

Some animals that live in this part of the world are not found anywhere else, such as the strange duck-billed platypus of Australia and the flightless kiwi of New Zealand. Animal farming is a big industry in Australia and New Zealand. There are many more sheep than people in both of these countries.

Blacktip reef shark

Butterfly fish

Great Barrier Reef

Blue-ringed octopus

Koala

Great Dividing Range

Duck-billed platypus

QUEENSLAND

Kookaburra

Darling

NEW SOUTH WALES

Blue-tongued skink

Murray

AUSTRALIAN CAPITAL TERRITORY

VICTORIA

Tasmanian devil

TASMANIA

Pacific Ocean

2

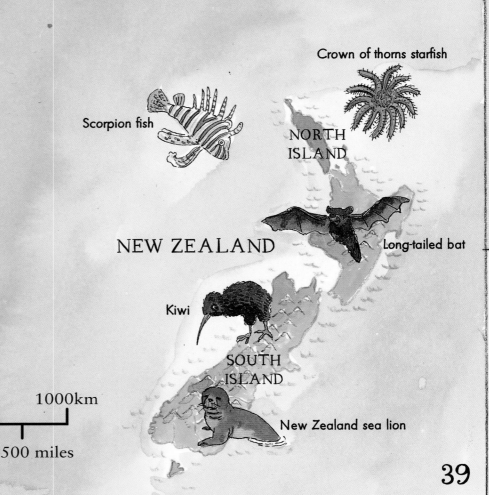

Crown of thorns starfish

Scorpion fish

NORTH ISLAND

3

Tasman Sea

NEW ZEALAND

Long-tailed bat

Kiwi

SOUTH ISLAND

New Zealand sea lion

4

0		1000km
0	500 miles	

40

THE PACIFIC ISLANDS

Thousands of tiny islands, home to lizards, birds, and insects, are scattered across the South Pacific Ocean. The tropical waters are full of fascinating ocean life.

Manta ray

Flying fish do not actually fly—they glide above the surface of the water on their outstretched fins. **Can you find one on the map?**

NORTHERN MARIANA ISLANDS (U.S.)

Anchovies

Sperm whale

Stonefish

MARSHALL ISLANDS

Blue marlin

2

FEDERATED STATES OF MICRONESIA

South Pacific Ocean

Key to countries:
1 GUAM (U.S.)
2 PALAU
3 NAURU
4 WALLIS & FUTUNA ISLANDS (FRANCE)
5 TOKELAU (N.Z.)
6 SAMOA
7 AMERICAN SAMOA (U.S.)
8 NIUE (N.Z.)
9 COOK ISLANDS (N.Z.)
10 PITCAIRN ISLANDS (U.K.)

Flying fish

Tree kangaroo

PAPUA NEW GUINEA

Leatherback turtle

KIRIBATI

Tahiti petrel

0   1000km

TUVALU

Honeyeater

0   500 miles

SOLOMON ISLANDS

VANUATU

Long-nosed sea horses

Banks flying fox

FIJI

FRENCH POLYNESIA (FRANCE)

3

NEW CALEDONIA (FRANCE)

Banded iguana

TONGA

Polynesian gecko

Giant squid

Great hammerhead shark

CORAL REEF

Coral reefs are formed with the shells of billions of tiny sea creatures. The Great Barrier Reef, which lies off the coast of northeast Australia, is home to a colorful collection of ocean life.

The **loggerhead turtle** eats clams, crabs, jellyfish, squid, and fish.

Spinner dolphins

The poisonous **olive sea snake** swims to the surface to breathe.

The poison of the **blue-ringed octopus** can kill an adult human in minutes.

Box jellyfish can grow as big as basketballs. They have a deadly sting.

Australian brain coral

Barrier reef anemonefish

Mandarin fish

Blue-spotted fantail ray

The **giant clam** is the world's largest mollusk. Its shell can be 5 feet (1.5 meters) long.

Clown fish

Pygmy sea horses

Blue starfish

Long-nosed butterfly fish

Tubular sponge

Staghorn coral

Sea cucumber

Sea urchin

41

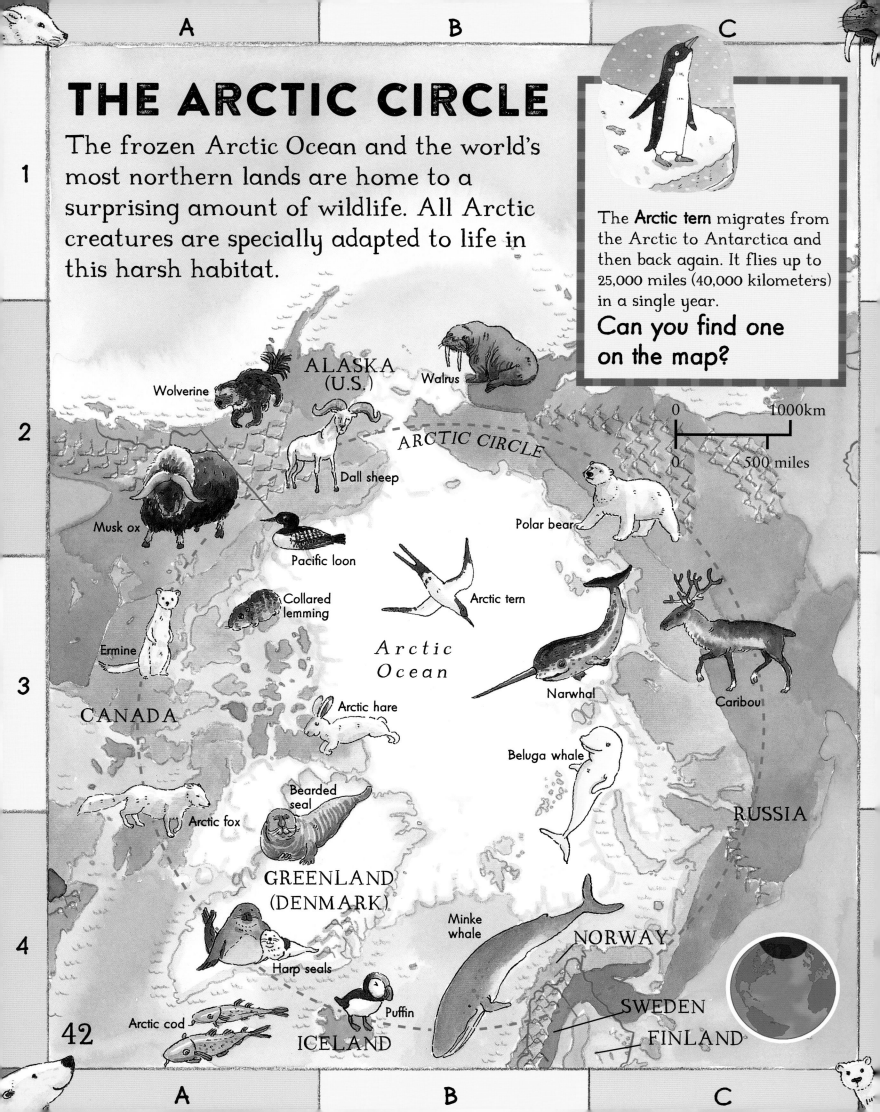

THE ARCTIC CIRCLE

The frozen Arctic Ocean and the world's most northern lands are home to a surprising amount of wildlife. All Arctic creatures are specially adapted to life in this harsh habitat.

The **Arctic tern** migrates from the Arctic to Antarctica and then back again. It flies up to 25,000 miles (40,000 kilometers) in a single year.

Can you find one on the map?

A   B   C

1

2

3

4

Wolverine

ALASKA (U.S.)

Walrus

Musk ox

Dall sheep

ARCTIC CIRCLE

Polar bear

0   1000km

0   500 miles

Pacific loon

Collared lemming

Arctic tern

Arctic Ocean

Ermine

Narwhal

Caribou

CANADA

Arctic hare

Beluga whale

RUSSIA

Arctic fox

Bearded seal

GREENLAND (DENMARK)

Minke whale

NORWAY

Harp seals

Puffin

Arctic cod

ICELAND

SWEDEN
FINLAND

42

ANTARCTICA

The continent of Antarctica is so cold that not many living things can survive there. Whales, sharks, and seals swim in the freezing waters, and penguins huddle together on the edges of the ice.

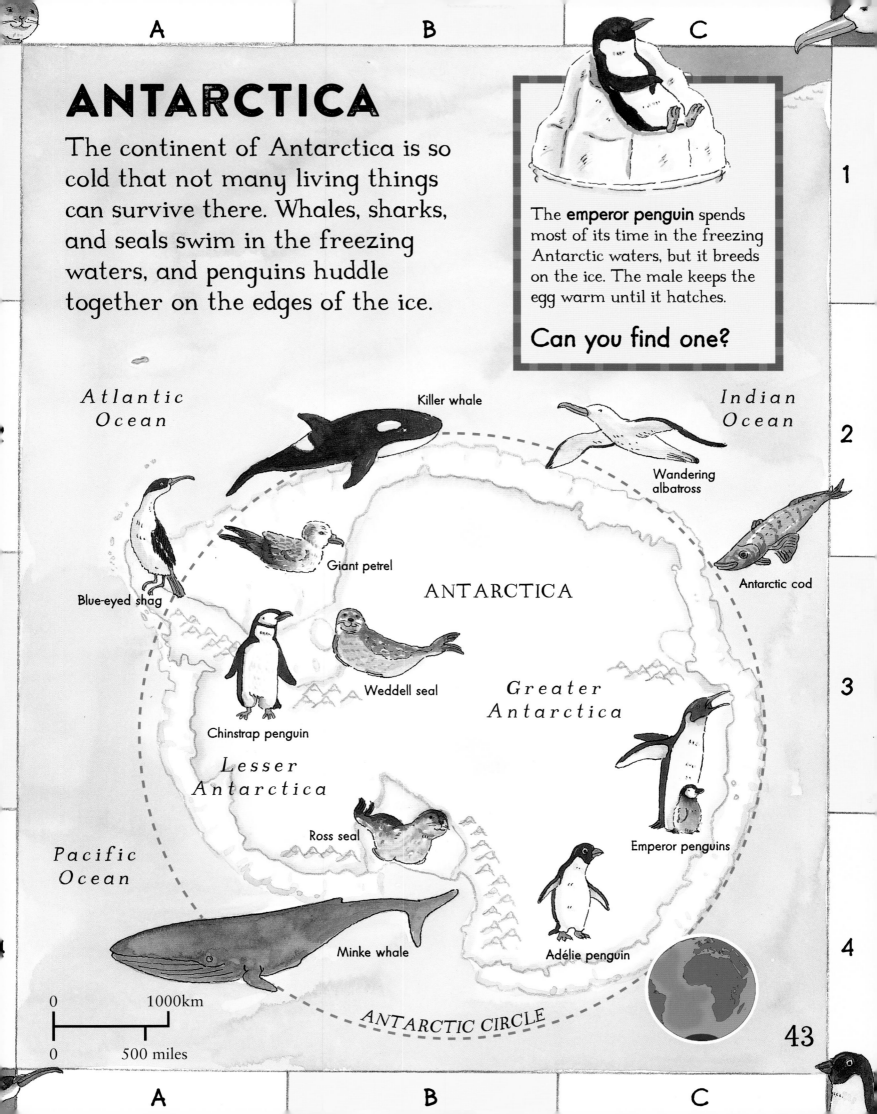

The **emperor penguin** spends most of its time in the freezing Antarctic waters, but it breeds on the ice. The male keeps the egg warm until it hatches.

Can you find one?

Killer whale

Atlantic Ocean

Indian Ocean

Wandering albatross

Giant petrel

Antarctic cod

ANTARCTICA

Blue-eyed shag

Weddell seal

Greater Antarctica

Chinstrap penguin

Lesser Antarctica

Pacific Ocean

Ross seal

Emperor penguins

Minke whale

Adélie penguin

0   1000km

0   500 miles

ANTARCTIC CIRCLE

A   B   C

A   B   C

1

2

3

4

THE ARCTIC

Very few plants grow in the freezing lands of the Arctic. A treeless plain, called the tundra, stretches out in all directions. At the coast, icy seawater laps against bare rocks and ice. Arctic animals have developed clever ways to stay safe and warm in their cold environment.

Beluga whale

The **narwhal** is a type of whale. Its tusk grows up to 10 feet (3 meters) long—around half the length of its body and tail.

The **walrus** has long tusks that it hooks onto ice so that it can sleep in the water.

Ringed seals are the most common seals in the Arctic. They are hunted by polar bears.

Northern collared lemmings

LEO, AN IMPRINT OF REGAN ARTS

FIRST REGAN ARTS HARDCOVER EDITION, 2022

LIBRARY OF CONGRESS CONTROL: 2021949862

ISBN 978-1-68245-193-9 (HARDCOVER)
ISBN 978-1-68245-194-6 (EBOOK)

INTERIOR DESIGN AND ILLUSTRATIONS BY DABIN HAN
COVER BY DABIN HAN

WWW.REGANARTS.COM
BROOKLYN | HOLLYWOOD

PRINTED IN CHINA